Original title:
Winter's Song

Author: Kaido Väinamäe
ISBN HARDBACK: 978-9908-1-1069-1
ISBN PAPERBACK: 978-9908-1-1070-7
ISBN EBOOK: 978-9908-1-1071-4

Echoing Crystals in the Dark

In the silence, shadows creep,
Whispers linger, secrets deep.
Crystals glint in muted light,
Echoes dance to calm the night.

Moonbeams weave through tangled trees,
Carrying tales on the breeze.
A symphony of soundless sighs,
Hearts unfold under starry skies.

Fractured dreams in glassy seams,
Reflecting all our hidden themes.
Shattered thoughts begin to mend,
In this dark, we find a friend.

Frosted edges, glimmering grace,
Each crystal holds a secret place.
Nature’s pulse in every shard,
Awakens truth that’s never hard.

In the dark, the echoes ring,
Carving silence, tales they bring.
A moment lost, yet found in night,
Where crystals glimmer, souls take flight.

Crystalline Cradle

In twilight's hush, the stars ignite,
A cradle formed of purest light.
Wrapped in dreams, we softly sway,
All worries fade, we drift away.

The moon hangs low, a silver thread,
Casting warmth where shadows tread.
In crystal silence, hearts entwine,
In this embrace, the world is thine.

The frosty air, a whispered song,
Echoes of where we belong.
Each breath a cloud, a fleeting trace,
In crystalline realms, we find our place.

Beneath the glow of night’s embrace,
Moments linger, time’s slow grace.
As stardust falls, we make our vow,
In this cradle, here and now.

So wrap me tight within your arms,
A refuge safe from all alarms.
In this stillness, love will bloom,
In crystalline light, we find our room.

Silence in the Depths of Snow

Falling flakes in softest white,
Blanket earth 'neath gentle night.
Whispers linger on the breeze,
Secrets hide among the trees.

The world transformed, a quiet sight,
Lost in dreams, we find our light.
Each step muffled, soft and slow,
In silence deep, the heart shall know.

Shadows dance on frosted ground,
In this peace, true solace found.
Not a sound, just pine and air,
Wrapped in winter's tender care.

The moon hangs high, a guiding glow,
Illuminating paths below.
As frost-kissed branches bend and sway,
In silence, winter holds its sway.

So let us wander, hand in hand,
Through this still and crystal land.
In the depths where snowflakes cling,
We’ll embrace what the silence brings.

Twilight's Icy Veil

The day surrenders to night’s call,
As twilight dances, shadows fall.
An icy veil wraps round the sky,
Where dreams awaken, hopes can fly.

Colors blend in a gentle hush,
As nature whispers in the rush.
With every breath, the world stands still,
A moment caught, a heart to fill.

The stars emerge, a silver glow,
In this twilight, secrets flow.
We walk through time, in soft embrace,
Within the veil, we find our place.

Frozen whispers catch the breeze,
Bearing tales of memories.
Underneath the fading light,
Love ignites the coming night.

So take my hand, let’s wander wide,
Through twilight’s grasp, we will glide.
In dreams of ice, with hearts so free,
Together, we'll weave our destiny.

Songs of Dappled Shadows

In the forest, sunlight plays,
Through leaves it weaves, a golden maze.
Among the trees, whispers call,
With dappled shadows, we embrace all.

The wind carries a gentle tune,
As nature hums beneath the moon.
A melody of life unfolds,
In every story, love retold.

Step softly on the forest's floor,
Where light and dark can’t help but soar.
Each moment shared, a fleeting dance,
In verdant realms, we dare to prance.

The colors blend, a painter’s dream,
In every glance, a spark, a gleam.
Through bough and branch, we find the way,
A symphony of night and day.

So linger here where shadows meet,
In harmony, our hearts repeat.
In the songs of dappled shade,
We'll find the love our souls have made.

The Art of Glacial Serenity

In whispers soft, the glaciers gleam,
A world untouched, a silent dream.
Each crevice holds a story still,
Time's handiwork, through frost and chill.

The air is pure, crisp and light,
A tranquil dance in morning's sight.
Mountains cradle a freezing lake,
Where peace resides, no hearts to break.

Beneath the azure, shadows play,
Frigid winds choose not to sway.
Every flake a unique trace,
Nature's art in frozen grace.

Out here, the whispers intertwine,
A symphony of space divine.
Each breath a gift from ages past,
In glacial calm, our souls hold fast.

From icy depths, wisdom flows,
In every crack, a secret knows.
Embrace the calm, let silence start,
The art refined, a frozen heart.

Echoes of Cozy Firesides

Amidst the crackle, laughter rings,
A world ignites, as warmth it brings.
Each ember glows, a memory made,
In cozy nooks where hearts won’t fade.

Stories shared, old tales retold,
The fire’s dance, a sight to behold.
With blankets drawn and spirits high,
We trace the stars in evening’s sky.

The scent of pine, a sweet embrace,
A gentle glow on every face.
Whispers blend with the night’s soft sigh,
In fireside's arms, time seems to fly.

Hot cocoa swirls in frosted mugs,
While laughter flies like playful hugs.
The world outside may chill and bite,
But here we bask in pure delight.

As shadows play, the flames will rise,
Reflections warm in friendly eyes.
Every crackle, a promise near,
In cozy fires, we conquer fear.

Veins of Ice Running Deep

In caverns cold, the icicles hang,
Silent rivers in frost’s sweet clang.
Through ancient paths, the whispers glide,
Veins of ice, the earth’s true pride.

Glacial flows pulse with life unknown,
Beneath the surface, stories are sewn.
Within the depths, where shadows creep,
The secrets lie, in silence deep.

Frost-kissed stones, a shimmering lace,
Each turn reveals a hidden place.
In icy heart, the whispers blend,
A timeless tale that has no end.

Beneath the weight of winter's hold,
Nature's art in blue and bold.
Veins of ice that shape the land,
A frozen world, so grand, so planned.

As daylight fades, the cold takes reign,
The beauty stirs, yet brings a strain.
For in the depths, both still and steep,
Are veins of ice, where spirits sleep.

Breathless Nights Beneath the Stars

Beneath the veil of velvet skies,
Endless dreams in starlight rise.
Each twinkling light, a story spun,
A silent pact with the setting sun.

The coolness of the night enfolds,
In whispered breaths, a spell unfolds.
The moon, our guide in silver dress,
Illuminates the world with finesse.

Each constellation, a path we trace,
In breathless wonder, we find our place.
With every sigh, we drift away,
Chasing echoes of night and day.

In quiet moments, whispers flow,
The cosmos sings, but few can know.
With hearts aligned to the universe,
We rise and fall, a cosmic verse.

As dawn approaches, stars take flight,
In new beginnings, we find the light.
Beneath the heavens, together we roam,
In breathless nights, we find our home.

Echoes of Snowflakes

Softly they dance, the snowflakes fall,
Whispers of winter, a silken call.
Each one unique, a tale to share,
Painting the world with frosted care.

In twilight's glow, they shimmer bright,
Drifting gently through the night.
Silent symphony, serene and pure,
Nature's artwork, a dream demure.

They kiss the ground, a gentle touch,
Transforming all, it means so much.
Layer by layer, they weave their quilt,
A canvas of white, softly built.

Under moon's gaze, they twinkle and gleam,
In the stillness, a poet's dream.
Echoes of snowflakes whispering low,
Of beauty found in the depths of snow.

Frost-kissed Reflections

In the still air, a chill does creep,
Frosty branches where secrets sleep.
Nature's mirror, a crystal sheen,
Reflections dance in silvered green.

Every dawn brings a jeweled sight,
Captured moments in morning light.
Gentle glimmers on every leaf,
Frost-kissed whispers, a beauty brief.

Frozen whispers in the brisk breeze,
Nature hums soft, aiming to please.
Hues of winter, a palette divine,
Frost-kissed reflections, perfectly shine.

In the quiet, a world unfolds,
Stories of winter in whispers told.
Embracing the chill, hearts thaw and breathe,
In frost-kissed moments, we dare to believe.

The Lullaby of Cold Nights

The stars above twinkle like dreams,
In the hush of night, cold softly beams.
Crickets sing low, their song a caress,
Wrapped in the warmth, we find our rest.

Snow blankets the earth, a gentle sigh,
While shadows glide beneath the sky.
The moonlight weaves through branches bare,
A lullaby sung with delicate care.

Clouds drift softly, like whispers of peace,
In the heart of winter, we find release.
Fires flicker low, as embers glow bright,
The lullaby of cold, a soothing night.

Dreams weave through the chill, softly spun,
As warmth wraps around, the day is done.
In the night's embrace, we close our eyes,
To the lullaby sung beneath the skies.

Hushed Footprints in the Snow

Footprints whisper in the pure white,
Every step a tale of delight.
In the silence, a story unfolds,
Hushed footsteps echo, secrets told.

A pathway carved in wintry grace,
Leading us to a sacred space.
Where laughter mingles with frostbit air,
In the stillness, there's magic to share.

Each print a moment, a memory made,
Stitched in time, they gently fade.
As the world spins on, and seasons flow,
Hushed footprints linger in the snow.

Beneath the sky, so vast and bright,
We follow our dreams in the soft moonlight.
With every step, we leave our mark,
In the hush of night, we ignite a spark.

A Symphony of Icy Breezes

Whispers of frost kiss the night,
Gentle caresses, purest white.
Stars twinkle like notes in the air,
Echoing secrets beyond compare.

Trees sway softly in winter's embrace,
Each branch adorned, a delicate lace.
Melodies dance on the shivering ground,
Nature's symphony, a beauty profound.

Through valleys where silent shadows creep,
The winds compose songs that lull to sleep.
Rhythms of cold in the vastness play,
A symphony crafted in silver gray.

In the heart of the chill, warmth is found,
Within the stillness, a pulse, a sound.
Each icy breeze tells a story bright,
Of winter's magic, the love for the night.

As dawn breaks, the song fades away,
Leaving whispers of dreams in the day.
Yet echoes remain, as sweet as can be,
In the symphony of the icy sea.

Shimmers of Crystal Dreams

Morning light weaves through the trees,
Dancing on leaves, a gentle tease.
Each droplet sparkles with pure delight,
A tapestry glimmers in the soft light.

Whispers of magic in the frosty air,
Nature unfolds a beauty rare.
Crystals shimmer with colors anew,
Reflecting the dreams that once flew.

Silhouettes cast by the sun's embrace,
Glistening pathways, a radiant lace.
Every step is a journey, serene,
In the landscape of shimmering sheen.

As day wanes, the world turns to gold,
Crystal dreams shimmer, a wonder to hold.
Fragrant breezes carry stories untold,
In the arms of twilight, our hopes unfold.

Beneath the moon's gaze, the magic gleams,
In every corner, where silence dreams.
These shimmers of light, forever they'll stay,
In the heart of the night, guiding the way.

Beneath the Silver Sky

Underneath the vast silver dome,
Whispers of night invite us home.
Stars flicker like our fading sighs,
Painting dreams beneath the silver skies.

Gentle breezes carry the night's tune,
A lullaby sung by the glowing moon.
Reflections cascade on the tranquil lake,
Where memories linger, and spirits awake.

Silhouettes dance in the twilight's grace,
As time captures each fleeting trace.
Beneath the canopy, serenity flows,
In the heartbeats of night, tranquility grows.

As horizons blend into shades of deep,
Nature cradles our souls in sleep.
In the stillness, connections arise,
Binding our hearts beneath the silver skies.

With every twinkle, our hopes ignite,
Guided by starbeams, weaving the night.
Together we dream, united and high,
In the embrace of the silver sky.

Frozen Hues of Dusk

Beneath the canvas of fading light,
Frozen hues awaken the night.
Purples blend with the softest blue,
Creating a vision, both wild and true.

As shadows stretch, they softly sway,
Painting the land at the close of day.
Each color whispers a story deep,
Of dreams held close, of promises to keep.

The horizon blushes; the stars come alive,
In the heart of dusk, our spirits thrive.
Every hue tells of a journey long,
Carried by whispers, our eternal song.

Chilled air dances on the edge of time,
Embracing silence like a gentle rhyme.
In the frozen dusk, the world stands still,
As nature weaves magic with every will.

With each passing moment, beauty we trust,
In frozen hues, turn dreams into dust.
Under twilight's gaze, we shall find,
The warmth of hope, forever intertwined.

The Stillness of a Snowfall

Softly it drapes the earth,
Whispers of winter's breath,
A velvety cloak of silence,
In stillness, we find rest.

Each flake dances, unique,
A ballet from the skies,
As time itself pauses,
And the world gently sighs.

Crisp air fills our lungs,
With each step, a crunch,
Nature wraps her treasures,
In a frosty, white bunch.

Branches bow with the weight,
Of glistening white crowns,
The beauty of this moment,
In the calm that surrounds.

Underneath this soft quilt,
The earth softens its call,
Embraced by winter’s magic,
In the stillness of all.

The Language of Frozen Sounds

In every hushed whisper,
The winter air speaks clear,
A melody of stillness,
That only hearts can hear.

Crackling underfoot,
A symphony unfolds,
Each step, a note of wonder,
As the silence enfolds.

Branches creak like old tales,
In the cold, crisp embrace,
Nature's song dances lightly,
In this enchanted space.

Frosty breaths rise in clouds,
A choral sigh of night,
Echoing through the valleys,
In the pale moonlight.

In this frozen concert,
Harmony reigns supreme,
A language of the winter,
Bound in nature's dream.

Enchanted Frost Underfoot

With each step, a sparkle,
Beneath my wandering feet,
Frost whispers its secrets,
Where land and magic meet.

The ground is a canvas,
Of each glittering hue,
Imprints tell stories,
That breeze softly blew.

Crisp shadows dressed in white,
Carve paths where I roam,
Footprints weave through dreams,
In this wintery home.

Whimsy fills the cool air,
As snowflakes swirl and twirl,
Each moment a treasure,
In this wintry whirl.

This enchanted realm sings,
A lullaby so sweet,
In the frost beneath me,
I find peace in each beat.

A Heartbeat Beneath the Snow

Beneath the blanket white,
Life quietly hums along,
A heartbeat hidden gently,
In a still, snowy song.

Nature finds her rhythm,
In the pulse of the cold,
Whispers of life thriving,
In stories untold.

The earth breathes an echo,
Beneath layers of frost,
Resilience in silence,
In the warmth, we aren't lost.

Each flake a soft promise,
Of what’s soon to return,
Beneath the snow's cover,
A flame waits to burn.

In this serene moment,
Life’s quiet glow takes flight,
A heartbeat beneath snow,
Fills the world with light.

The Purity of Moonlit Snow

Under the moon's soft, silver glow,
Blankets of snow, a gentle flow.
Footprints vanish, lost in white,
Whispers of peace embrace the night.

Stars above twinkle and play,
Guiding lost dreams, come what may.
Each flake dances, unique in grace,
Nature's canvas, a tranquil space.

Trees stand tall, cloaked in light,
Branches heavy, a wondrous sight.
Silence reigns, a soothing balm,
In stillness, we find our calm.

Frosted breath, the air is crisp,
Every moment, we gently grasp.
With every glance, hearts beat slow,
In the purity of moonlit snow.

Embracing beauty, wild and free,
A world transformed, a memory.
Beneath the night's soft, silken thread,
Whispered secrets, softly said.

Hibernation's Gentle Call

In the heart of winter's sleep,
Nature whispers, soft and deep.
Creatures nestle, all around,
In cozy burrows, peace is found.

Snowflakes blanket, a calming scene,
In the stillness, all is serene.
Time slows down, the world turns white,
Cradled close through the long night.

Dreams drift softly on frosty air,
Hibernation's embrace, a gentle care.
Stories of spring linger near,
In every sigh, anticipation clear.

Moonlit nights weave silver threads,
As stillness tugs at sleepy heads.
Life awaits beneath the snow,
Ready to awaken, grow, and glow.

Cycles turn, a dance so slow,
In slumber's arms, we learn to glow.
Nature's rhythm, a soothing call,
Hibernation's warmth envelops all.

Silent Whispers of Frost

Frosted mornings, whispers soft,
A quiet world beneath skies aloft.
Glistening jewels on branches bare,
A tapestry woven with delicate care.

Each breath released, a vapor trail,
Spirits dance in winter's veil.
The earth holds secrets, hushed, profound,
In icy grips, life still surrounds.

Footsteps crunch on frozen ground,
Silent stories await, unbound.
With every step, a tale unfolds,
Of winter's magic, brave and bold.

Underneath the frost, dreams reside,
Awaiting warmth, where hope can glide.
Silent whispers fill the air,
Winter's song, a tender prayer.

In the chill, we pause and listen,
To nature's voice, soft and glisten.
Frost embraces, gently holds,
In silent whispers, magic unfolds.

Chilling Melodies of the North

From towering peaks to valleys low,
Chilling melodies, whispers flow.
Winds of winter, chorus grand,
Nature sings across the land.

Rustling leaves and icy streams,
Echoes of ancient, frozen dreams.
Mountains ring with harmony,
In the chill, souls fly free.

Boreal forests, shadows dance,
Creatures stir, lost in a trance.
With every howl, the night ignites,
A symphony beneath the lights.

Northern lights, a vibrant glow,
Painting skies with colors flow.
In this realm, the magic swirls,
Chilling melodies of winter's pearls.

Beyond the frost, hearts start to thaw,
Each note a gift, a sacred law.
In the north, where spirits soar,
Chilling melodies forevermore.

Frosted Whispers

In the hush of winter's breath,
Frosted whispers fill the air.
Trees stand still, a quiet death,
Nature wrapped in a silver layer.

Moonlight glimmers on the snow,
Casting shadows, silken white.
Footsteps soft, where few may go,
Hidden secrets in the night.

Silent dreams beneath the frost,
Moments caught in whispered glee.
Time stands still, no love is lost,
In this realm, it's just you and me.

Crystal flakes like diamonds fall,
Each one telling tales anew.
Nature’s canvas, great and small,
In the frost, a world so true.

The night's embrace, both warm and cold,
Awakens wonder, pure delight.
In frosted whispers, stories told,
Held in silence, soft and light.

Chills Beneath the Moon

Underneath the chilling glow,
The moon whispers secrets clear.
Shadows dance with ebb and flow,
Wrapped in winter’s quiet cheer.

A breath of cold on glowing cheeks,
Winds that carry tales untamed.
In these nights, the silence speaks,
Of ancient dreams we’ve almost claimed.

Stars like diamonds dot the sky,
Glimmers soft on snowy ground.
As the wintry breezes sigh,
Magic lingers all around.

Each tremor of the frosty air,
Brings a shiver down my spine.
Moments frozen, memories rare,
All the magic feels divine.

In stillness, hearts begin to stir,
Wrapped in beauty’s hushed embrace.
Underneath this moon’s soft purr,
We find solace, time and space.

Echoes of Silent Nights

In the depth of silent nights,
Echoes drift on icy streams.
Whispers soft, like fragile lights,
Illuminate our hidden dreams.

Moonlight bathes the world in grey,
Crystals glinting in the dark.
Nature holds the night at bay,
In this stillness, sparks a spark.

Footsteps crunch on winter's crust,
Every sound a sweet embrace.
In the night, we place our trust,
Lost in time's alluring grace.

Chill winds breathe a soft refrain,
Carrying tales of the past.
Filling hearts with gentle pain,
Echoes of what will not last.

Yet in quiet, hope ignites,
Through the dark, we find our way.
In the magic of these nights,
Love will guide us, come what may.

Snowflakes Dance and Twirl

Snowflakes dance and twirl around,
In a whirlwind, soft and light.
Nature's beauty, veil profound,
Wrapping earth in purest white.

Each one falls with grace untold,
Spiraling through the starry night.
Delicate and bright as gold,
They shimmer in the moon’s soft light.

Children laugh, their faces bright,
Chasing dreams in drifts so deep.
In the chill of crisp twilight,
Winter's magic steals our sleep.

Catch a flake upon your tongue,
Taste the cold that winter brings.
In this season, hearts are young,
As the snow falls, joy takes wings.

So let the snowflakes sway and spin,
Paint the world in frosty cheer.
In their dance, new ties begin,
Whispers of love for all to hear.

The Warmth of Old Memories

Whispers linger in the air,
Soft laughter fills the room,
Faded photographs laid bare,
Recalling joy beyond the gloom.

Childhood dreams in gentle light,
Echoes of a time long past,
Familiar faces, hearts so bright,
In our minds, their shadows cast.

The scent of baked goods wafts through,
A cup of tea, a shared embrace,
Heartstrings pull, emotions brew,
In this sacred, cherished space.

Fireside tales, both old and new,
A thread that binds us, strong yet frail,
Moments stitched in vintage hue,
A tapestry of love's sweet tale.

As twilight dims, memories glimmer,
In the heart, they softly flame,
Through passing years, they only shimmer,
Forever etched, they still remain.

An Ascent through Frozen Woods

Snowflakes fall like whispered dreams,
Muted whispers fill the air,
Trees stand proud, silvered beams,
Nature’s hush, a tranquil prayer.

Footsteps crunch on icy ground,
A solitary path I trace,
In this silence, peace is found,
The frozen realm, my heart’s embrace.

Frosted branches, nature’s lace,
Reflecting light in crystal gleam,
Chasing shadows, curious grace,
One with winter’s frozen seam.

The chill wraps me in its arms,
As I climb, the summit’s near,
In the stillness, subtle charms,
Woods alive, whispering clear.

Reaching heights, the world expands,
Winds sing tales from faraway,
Nature’s grandeur, carved by hands,
In this moment, I must stay.

Embracing the Nowhere Nights

Stars sprinkle across the night,
A tapestry of endless dreams,
In the stillness, hearts take flight,
Embracing all the silent themes.

Whispers glide on midnight air,
The moon, a guardian so bright,
Time stands still, without a care,
Wrapped in shadows, soft and light.

Crisp and cool, the breeze invites,
Thoughts drift aimlessly, untamed,
Lost among the timeless sights,
In the darkness, hopes proclaimed.

Moments stretch, a soothing balm,
In this nowhere, peace aligns,
Embracing chaos, finding calm,
Where the world and soul combines.

Dreams unfold beneath the stars,
Each heartbeat echoes in the night,
Within the quiet, mending scars,
In a realm of pure delight.

Tundra's Requiem

Endless stretches under skies,
Where snow and silence intertwine,
The tundra breathes, deep and wise,
Glimmers of life, a stark design.

Whispers ride the icy breeze,
Beneath the frost, a tale unfolds,
Of nature's strength, bending trees,
In frozen beauty, life beholds.

Colors fade, yet still they call,
Soft hues beneath the shining sun,
A delicate dance, the snowflakes fall,
In this realm, the sacred run.

Ethereal sights, a ghostly hue,
Echoes of those who braved the chill,
Their stories weave like threads of blue,
In my heart, they linger still.

Yet through the cold, a warmth we find,
In the quiet, life holds its breath,
In heartbeats shared, a bond defined,
Tundra whispers songs of death.

A Reverie in Hibernation

In the quiet of the night,
A blanket soft and white,
Dreams weave through the still air,
While the world rests unaware.

Whispers of the snowflakes fall,
Embracing trees, peaceful call,
Wrapped in warmth, the earth sleeps,
As the gentle silence creeps.

Time moves slow in frozen glow,
Nature's rhythm, soft and slow,
A lullaby of winter's grace,
Creating magic in this space.

Under stars that twinkle bright,
Hope ignites the dark of night,
Each moment swells with peace,
In this tranquil masterpiece.

Awake soon, the world will stir,
For now, in dreams, we purr,
Hibernation's quiet song,
Whispers softly, all night long.

Dreams of the Frosted Twilight

In twilight's grip, the world transforms,
With silver light in softest forms,
Frosted whispers kiss the ground,
In quietude, beauty's found.

As shadows stretch and colors fade,
The landscape dons a crystal cloak laid,
Dreams dance in the freezing air,
Unfolding hopes, both bright and rare.

Hushed are the giggles of the breeze,
Among the whispers of frozen trees,
Every flake a tale to tell,
In this wonderland, all is well.

Stars awaken, shyly peeking,
Casting wishes, gently speaking,
In each frosted breath we share,
The magic lingers everywhere.

As night enfolds this tranquil scene,
A tapestry of silver glean,
We cradled dreams that spark the night,
In frosted twilight's soft delight.

Twinkling Stars Over Silent Snow

Under a canvas, vast and deep,
Stars twinkle while the world sleeps,
Snowflakes drift, a silent hush,
In this stillness, hearts will rush.

Each shimmer tells a tale untold,
Of dreams and wishes, brave and bold,
The night unfolds a velvet cue,
A dance that's ancient, pure, and true.

Frosted branches catch the light,
Whispers echo through the night,
In this quiet, love will grow,
Beneath stars over silent snow.

The earth breathes softly, wrapped in white,
As shadows linger in the night,
A timeless bond, a memory's glow,
In harmony, we come to know.

In winter's heart, we find our place,
Within the calm, we weave our grace,
Forever bound, as stars bestow,
Their light above the silent snow.

Veils of Frost Under Moonlight

Veils of frost on grass do gleam,
Draped in the softest moonlit dream,
Whispers ripple through the night,
Gentle shadows, silver light.

Beneath the glow, the world awaits,
As time unfolds and gently creates,
A tapestry of winter's weave,
In every moment, we believe.

The crisp air carries laughter's song,
As nature's pulse beats deep and strong,
Frost-kissed petals shine so bright,
Guided by the stars in flight.

Underneath this vast expanse,
Magic twirls in every glance,
Every breath, a secret shared,
In moonlit night, we are ensnared.

So let us dance in silver beams,
In quiet spaces where hope gleams,
Veils of frost on this serene sight,
Embraced forever by the night.

Nature’s Quiet Reverie

Whispers of the morning breeze,
Gentle rustle through the trees.
Soft sunlight paints the ground,
In this peace, a joy is found.

Dewdrops glisten on the grass,
Time, like clouds, begins to pass.
Birds compose their morning song,
Nature’s voice, both sweet and strong.

Butterflies dance on vibrant hues,
Flitting softly, sharing news.
Every petal, every leaf,
Offers solace, sweet belief.

Mountains cradle skies so wide,
In their shadows, dreams abide.
Rivers flow with softest grace,
Nature beckons, a warm embrace.

As the sun begins to dip,
Colors blend in twilight's grip.
This quietude, a sacred space,
In nature’s heart, we find our place.

A Dance of Crystal Traces

Frosted whispers on the pane,
Each one tells a tale of rain.
Icicles hang like chandeliers,
Catching light, dispelling fears.

Footprints mark the snowy trail,
Leading onward, like a sail.
Children laugh, their joy ablaze,
As they weave through winter's maze.

Clouds above in shades of gray,
Yet beneath, the cold can't stay.
Nature dances, sparkles bright,
In the stillness of the night.

Trees stand tall, adorned with white,
Guardians of the silent night.
Every branch, a work of art,
Capturing winter's beating heart.

As the moonlight starts to glow,
Crystal tracings start to show.
In this magic, we discover,
The beauty in the cold’s soft cover.

A Glimpse of Solstice Shadows

Longer nights and shorter days,
Nature's breath in twilight plays.
Shadows stretch across the land,
Painting stories, bold and grand.

Golden hues of fading light,
Crickets sing to greet the night.
Stars emerge, a silent choir,
Illuminating dreams' desire.

Winter’s chill, a soft embrace,
Blanketing the earth's wide face.
The world hushed in quiet grace,
In shadows, we find our place.

Trees sway gently, whispers low,
Carrying secrets only they know.
Moonlight weaves a silver thread,
Through the dreams that softly spread.

With each breath, the world appears,
A tapestry of hopes and fears.
In these shadows, softly cast,
We glimpse futures, bright and vast.

The Heartbeat of the Winter Woods

In the stillness, whispers call,
Nature's heartbeat, felt by all.
Crunch of snow beneath our feet,
Echoes pure in cold retreat.

Winds carry tales from afar,
Guiding dreams beneath the stars.
Each tree stands a sentinel,
Guarding secrets, holding well.

Pine and cedar, evergreen,
In their presence, calm is seen.
Branches bow with heavy snow,
Nature's rhythm, soft and slow.

Shadowed paths invite the soul,
Leading onward, making whole.
In the woods, where spirits glide,
Life's soft pulse, forever tied.

With each heartbeat, stories share,
Resonating through the air.
In winter's woods, we find our dreams,
Flowing like the mountain streams.

The Stillness of Distant Mountains

Mountains rise, their tips like dreams,
Silent guards, shrouded in beams.
Whispers of wind caress the stone,
In their stillness, the world feels alone.

Clouds drift by in a gentle dance,
Casting shadows in a fleeting glance.
The air is crisp, the sky so vast,
A tranquil moment, forever to last.

Valleys below, a tapestry spread,
Nature's wonders, the path we tread.
Colors blend in an artist's hand,
Each peak a poem, bold and grand.

The sun dips low, the day takes flight,
Mountains blush in the fading light.
Each silhouette a tale they tell,
In the distance, where spirits dwell.

Whispers linger long into night,
Under stars that shine so bright.
The stillness reigns, a soothing balm,
In the mountains, where hearts feel calm.

Candlelight against the Chill

In the dark, a flicker burns,
Softly glowing, the flame returns.
Candlelight dances, shadows sway,
Chasing cold and night away.

Glow of amber, warm embrace,
In its light, we find our place.
Flickering whispers, secrets shared,
In quiet hours, no one spared.

Outside winds howl with icy breath,
Yet here we find a spark from death.
Candlelight fights against the freeze,
A beacon shining, aiming to please.

Thoughts drift like smoke, swirling high,
In its warmth, we laugh and cry.
Moments captured in the glow,
Heartfelt memories, all aglow.

As the night wears on, we hold tight,
The flame a friend, a guiding light.
Candlelight flickers, never still,
Against the chill, it bends to will.

Silver Threads of Winter's Embrace

Winter weaves its silver thread,
Blanketing fields, where soft dreams tread.
Tree branches shimmer, crystal lace,
Nature’s art, a flawless grace.

Footprints deep in snowbanks lie,
Whispers echo, a soft sigh.
The world slows, in stillness bound,
A peaceful hush, where souls are found.

Frosty breath in the morning air,
Promises linger, everywhere.
The bite of cold, a kiss so sweet,
In winter's hold, our hearts still beat.

Stars twinkle bright in a velvet dome,
Under this sky, we find our home.
Each flake a wish from heavens above,
Sprinkling magic, warmth, and love.

Glistening paths, a journey unfolds,
As stories of winter quietly told.
In silver threads, we dance and glide,
With winter's embrace, we take each stride.

The Heartbeat of Ice

Beneath the surface, rhythms dwell,
The heartbeat of ice, a silent swell.
Cracks and creaks, a soothing sound,
In frozen realms, life’s pulse is found.

Glacial rivers, slow and grand,
Moving gently, sculpting the land.
With each thaw, a whisper begins,
Awakening dreams that winter spins.

Underneath layers, secrets keep,
Where shadows dance and wonders sleep.
An ancient story carved in frost,
A treasure of time that isn't lost.

Icicles hang like crystal spears,
Collecting memories of our years.
In silence, the heartbeat echoes true,
A symphony crafted anew.

As spring approaches, the ice will break,
Revealing life in each fresh wake.
Yet in the stillness, a truth we know,
The heartbeat of ice will always flow.

Chasing the Ghosts of Sunlight

In the morning's soft embrace,
Shadows linger, hesitant to leave.
Whispers dance between the trees,
Chasing sunlight, a fleeting weave.

Golden rays stretch through the mist,
Illuminating paths we roam.
Every step, a gentle wish,
To find the warmth of a lost home.

Clouds drift by like dreams once bright,
Painting skies with hues of gold.
We run, we laugh, into the light,
Chasing tales of courage bold.

But twilight falls with a quiet sigh,
Resting dreams on tomorrow's brow.
Yet in our hearts, the light won't die,
Forever chasing, here and now.

So we gather up the sighs,
Turn them into hopeful beams.
As long as we keep our eyes,
We'll chase those sunlight dreams.

A Tapestry Woven with Silence

In the stillness of the night,
Words unspoken fill the air.
Threads of thought and silent flight,
We weave together all we share.

Fingers trace the patterns bold,
With every stitch, a memory made.
Colors blend, both bright and cold,
Each shadow on this tapestry laid.

Underneath the starry veil,
Whispers linger, deep and clear.
Every moment tells a tale,
Woven closely, year by year.

The fabric tells of love and loss,
Of journeys crossed and paths untold.
In silence, we feel, we assess
The stories deep in every fold.

So let us bask in this serene,
In the quiet, heartbeats blend.
A tapestry of what has been,
With silence, we learn to mend.

The Color of Frosted Dreams

In the morning frost we find,
Dreams like crystals, cold and bright.
Glistening softly, intertwined,
In the hush of winter's light.

With every breath, a gentle chill,
Awakening to magic’s glow.
Painting skies and valleys still,
The world adorned with purest snow.

Beneath the ice, the hopes await,
Emerging slowly, strong and clear.
Frosted wishes, a delicate fate,
Whispering secrets, drawing near.

As we wander through this scene,
Grasping moments, fleeting beams.
In the heart of winter’s sheen,
We chase the color of our dreams.

Together we tread softly on,
In the silence, warmth ignites.
Frosted dreams will never be gone,
Their brilliance sparks on shivering nights.

Chords of the Chilling Gale

In the howling night's embrace,
A chilling gale begins to weave.
Echoes dance in empty space,
With each note, the shadows breathe.

The moonlight bends to hear the song,
A melody both soft and bright.
It carries whispers, deep and long,
Cascading through the velvet night.

Branches sway beneath the strain,
As nature holds its breath, alive.
Each chord a memory, a pain,
In the winds, old ghosts survive.

Through the dark, a haunting tune,
Reverberates in every heart.
Underneath the silver moon,
The chilling gale plays its part.

Yet in the frost, we find our cheer,
With every note, we bravely sail.
Together, facing every fear,
Harmonizing with the chilling gale.

Silence Wrapped in Snow

Gentle flakes fall down, so white,
Covering the world, pure and bright.
Silent whispers fill the air,
In this stillness, peace we share.

Footprints vanish, soft and slow,
In the hush of winter's glow.
Branches bow and hold their weight,
Nature sleeps; it's never late.

The moon peers down, a silver hue,
A blanket wraps the earth anew.
Stars twinkle, shy above,
A tranquil world, we're blessed to love.

As time stands still, in soft embrace,
We find our thoughts in this sacred space.
Silence speaks in the cold night air,
Wrapped in snow, we find our care.

Soft Chimes of the Frosted Earth

Winter's breath, a gentle song,
Echoes where the trees grow strong.
Frosty whispers, chimes so clear,
Nature's music fills the near.

Sparkling crystals dance with light,
In the chill of silent night.
Branches sway in soft refrain,
A melody that breaks the pain.

Footsteps crunch on icy ground,
In this harmony, peace is found.
Every sound, a note divine,
In the frosted air, we align.

Snowflakes twirl, a bright ballet,
Nature's art in sheer display.
Soft chimes call from trees that sway,
A winter's hymn to greet the day.

The Whispering Pines

In the forest, tall they stand,
Whispering secrets, hand in hand.
Softly swaying in the breeze,
Nature's voices, gentle tease.

Their needles dance in light's embrace,
A sacred bond, a timeless place.
Echoing tales of days gone by,
Underneath the vast, clear sky.

With every rustle, stories told,
Of seasons changing, brave and bold.
The whispers weave a tapestry,
In emerald shades, wild and free.

As shadows stretch, they softly sigh,
A lullaby as stars drift by.
In the night, their breaths align,
Together, we converse in time.

Echoes of the Frozen Lake

On the frozen, glassy sheet,
Reflections dance, a chill so sweet.
Echoes ripple through the ice,
A haunting beauty, cold as dice.

Crackling sounds, the whispers call,
Of winter's grip that binds us all.
Silent stories, depths concealed,
In every wave, a truth revealed.

Underneath, the world sleeps tight,
Dreaming of the sun's warm light.
The frozen surface holds the past,
Memories of seasons that flew fast.

As twilight descends, shadows play,
Nature's canvas, a soft ballet.
Echoes linger, calling near,
In this stillness, all is clear.

The Chill of Twilight’s Breath

The sun dips low, the sky turns gray,
A whisper lingers, night holds sway.
Cool air wraps round like a cloak of mist,
The day retreats, a quiet tryst.

Shadows deepen, stars ignite,
In solitude, the world feels right.
Twilight breathes a secret sigh,
Painting dreams across the sky.

Crickets sing in a gentle tune,
Soon the rise of the silver moon.
A soft rustle in the trees,
Nature's breath upon the breeze.

With fading light, the stillness grows,
Embracing whispers, the evening glows.
Within the pause, the heart will find,
A sanctuary of the mind.

As twilight falls and shadows blend,
In every end, there's space to mend.
The chill of dusk, a tender thread,
Weave into dreams where hope is bred.

Winter’s Serenade in Silence

Snowflakes dance in the frosty air,
Whispers of winter everywhere.
Each flake brings a tale untold,
A serenade, both soft and cold.

Bare trees stand like silent guards,
Watching over slumbering yards.
In the hush, the world holds still,
Wrapped in a blanket, gentle chill.

Footprints echo on the path,
Each step a hint of winter's math.
Shadows stretch as daylight wanes,
In this peace, the spirit gains.

Sipping warmth from mugs of cheer,
Family gathers, laughter near.
In the stillness, hearts ignite,
A winter’s serenade, pure delight.

Fires crackle, stories unfold,
Moments cherished, memories bold.
Winter's whisper speaks so clear,
In silence found, love's warmth appears.

Songs of the Snowbound

Through the windows, white drifts lay,
A frosty world, in soft array.
Snowbound whispers, voices weave,
In the quiet, hearts believe.

As branches bow with weighty grace,
Time slows down in this sacred space.
Each snowflake holds a secret song,
Melodies where we belong.

Children laugh, they spin and glide,
In winter's arms, joy can't hide.
Creatures stir in their snowy dens,
Life goes on, as nature sends.

Beneath the blanket, all is still,
Nature resting, time to heal.
With every flake, stories share,
Songs of the snowbound fill the air.

Evening falls, the world aglow,
A hush descends on fields below.
Songs of the snowy night will play,
A tranquil dream till break of day.

Frosted Lullabies from the Hearth

Crackling flames in the hearth's embrace,
Frosted windows, a cozy place.
Each ember glows, a flickering light,
Whispers of warmth on a chilly night.

Blankets wrapped, stories unfold,
Lullabies of winter, softly told.
In the glow of the fire's breath,
We find solace, defying death.

The world outside, a glistening show,
Twinkling lights, a frosty glow.
Inside, the laughter dances bright,
Frosted lullabies, pure delight.

Gingerbread scents fill the air,
Love and warmth crafted with care.
In this moment, everything's clear,
The magic of winter, so near.

As night deepens, stars gleam in sight,
Frosted dreams take wondrous flight.
With hearts aglow, we hold what's dear,
Lullabies of winter, ever near.

Muffled Laughter in the Dark

Whispers of joy in shadows creep,
Silence surrounds, secrets we keep.
Echoes of giggles, soft and low,
In the night where friendships grow.

Under the moon's watchful gaze,
Laughter dances in friendly haze.
Moments shared in serene disguise,
Beneath the stars, our spirits rise.

The world outside fades into black,
But in this warmth, there's no lack.
Soft breaths mingle with the air,
In this haven, free from care.

Flickers of light, fireflies play,
Guiding our hearts in a gentle sway.
In the dark, bonds we weave tight,
Muffled laughter sparks the night.

As dawn approaches, shadows blend,
Memories linger, never end.
In the quiet, our hearts unite,
In the dark, a precious light.

Stars Adorned in Ice

Glistening gems on velvet skies,
Whispering secrets, ancient ties.
Each star a dream, a glimmering thought,
In the chill, a warmth that's sought.

Frozen breath paints the night air,
Hints of magic, everywhere.
Twinkling lights in the cold reside,
Nature's quilt, a celestial guide.

Like diamonds scattered on dark seas,
Sparkling bright with every freeze.
These distant flames, so pure and wise,
Watch over us with watchful eyes.

Underneath this icy dome,
Each shining light calls us home.
In the stillness, we find our peace,
As frosted whispers softly cease.

The night wraps us in its embrace,
In every star, a sacred space.
Together we dream, with hearts entwined,
In the vastness, our souls aligned.

Glacial Echoes of Solitude

In the stillness, mountains sigh,
Whispers of ice as time goes by.
Frigid winds carve the silent stone,
Echoes of solitude, never alone.

The world retreats, a quiet cocoon,
Beneath the watchful, silver moon.
Footsteps crunch on freshly fallen snow,
Tracing paths where few dare go.

Frostbitten branches softly sway,
In nature's grip, we drift away.
Time slows down, a breath released,
In solitude, chaos finds peace.

Crystals hang from every bough,
Nature's art, we humbly bow.
Each glacial echo, a story told,
In the heart of silence, bold and cold.

Here we find our thoughts laid bare,
Wrapped in a world of frozen air.
In echoes deep, our spirits play,
In solitude, we drift away.

A Tapestry of Chilling Breezes

Leaves whisper tales to passing gales,
A dance of shadows, nature's trails.
Each breath of wind a story spun,
In chilling breezes, life's woven fun.

Through swaying trees, emotions flow,
In twilight's grasp, the cool winds blow.
Whistling softly, secrets share,
Weaving dreams in the evening air.

Each breeze carries a touch of frost,
In this world where warmth seems lost.
Yet within the cold, a spark remains,
A tapestry formed of joys and pains.

Glimmers of hope in the dark night,
Hold onto dreams, embrace the light.
For in the chill, connections thrive,
In each breeze, the heart's alive.

So let the winds sing their refrain,
In the dance of life, joy and pain.
Together we weave, with hearts that seize,
A tapestry spun from chilling breezes.

Veils of Misty Eyes

In twilight's grasp, the shadows weave,
A tapestry of dreams one can believe.
Soft whispers brush the silent trees,
As moonlight dances on the gentle breeze.

Ghostly shapes in dusky light,
Call the stars to take their flight.
Each breath a sigh, a fleeting sound,
In this serene world, peace is found.

Fading colors of the day,
Breathe in wonder, fade away.
Veils of mist in colors spun,
Eve's soft glories have begun.

All around, the night unfolds,
Stories whispered, secrets told.
In gentle hush, the world sleeps tight,
Wrapped in the arms of soft twilight.

Magic lingers, hearts in thrall,
In misty eves where shadows fall.
With every gust, the night awakes,
In this embrace, the spirit takes.

Choral Echoes of Solitude

In the silence, a soft refrain,
Melodies of joy, tinged with pain.
Voices rise like the morning dew,
Choral echoes, pure and true.

Underneath the weeping sky,
Solitude sings, a gentle sigh.
Harmony lingers in the air,
A symphony of quiet care.

In every note, a story spun,
Of lost loves and battles won.
Each echo finds a path to roam,
In solitude, we find our home.

Stars above hum along the tune,
Brushing dreams like a silver moon.
In the stillness, hearts entwine,
Choral whispers, divine design.

Resting softly in the night,
Solitude glows, a gentle light.
In the choral echoes, we find grace,
A tranquil heart, a sacred space.

Frosty Fir Trees in Harmony

In the forest, the firs stand tall,
Draped in frost, the winter's shawl.
Whispers of wind through branches weave,
Nature's song, one can't believe.

Crystalline flakes gently fall,
Kissing the ground, a fairytale call.
Frosty limbs in the pale moonlight,
Guarding secrets of the night.

With every breath, a cloud appears,
Echoing warmth, dispelling fears.
In this haven, the world feels right,
Harmony glows, pure and bright.

Silent nights under starlit skies,
Where every crystal secretly lies.
Firs standing proud, a noble view,
Each adorned with dreams anew.

Together they whisper, a soft embrace,
Guardians of time and sacred space.
In frost's embrace, they celebrate,
Nature's bond, an endless fate.

The Language of Snowflakes

Delicate dancers fall from above,
Each snowflake whispers tales of love.
Unique patterns, a fleeting art,
Nature’s letters that warm the heart.

A quiet hush blankets the eve,
In winter’s grasp, we all believe.
Soft landings on a waiting ground,
In their silence, joy is found.

Every flake a story told,
Of frosty nights and days of gold.
They drift and swirl, a soft ballet,
Painting the world in a dreamy way.

Underneath the silver glow,
The language speaks as breezes blow.
A rhythm found in chilled embrace,
The art of winter, a soft grace.

In crystal shapes, the world stands still,
Embracing magic, hearts to fill.
For in each flake lies mystery,
The language of snowflakes, wild and free.

Sonnet of the Fading Sun

The sun dips low, a golden hue,
Casting shadows on the ground.
With every breath, the evening's due,
A silent hush, a gentle sound.

Fingers of light stretch far and wide,
Embracing waves of twilight's grace.
Nature sighs, a soothing tide,
As darkness claims its rightful space.

The clouds, like dreams, begin to fade,
Painting skies in hues of blue.
In the stillness, memories laid,
Of warmth that once embraced the view.

Time whispers softly, shadows grow,
As stars awaken, one by one.
And in the night's serene tableau,
We bid farewell to the fading sun.

The Gentle Touch of Frost

A veil of white upon the dawn,
Each blade adorned, a crystal crown.
The world, in slumber, lightly drawn,
Awaits the warmth, as winter's gown.

The breath of winter, crisp and clear,
Leaves whispers on the quiet air.
Beneath the trees, the chill draws near,
A dance of silence, soft and rare.

Tread lightly on this frosty ground,
For nature sleeps, a dream in sight.
In every corner, beauty found,
Reflecting whispers of the night.

With every shimmer, time stands still,
As stars peek through the cloak of gray.
A gentle touch, a quiet thrill,
In moments fleeting, night turns day.

Whispers Beneath the Ice

Beneath the layer, still and deep,
Whispers linger, soft and light.
The world above may drift in sleep,
Yet life persists in hidden night.

Crystal caverns, secrets hide,
In silence, stories slowly breathe.
A dance of shadows comes alive,
As ancient roots begin to weave.

Echoes call from depths obscure,
Where time and memory entwine.
Each pulse, a heartbeat, strong and pure,
Preserving tales both lost and fine.

Frozen whispers weave their thread,
In chilly breaths of silver blue.
A tapestry of life widespread,
Beneath the ice, old dreams renew.

Melodies of the Shivering Stars

In the velvet sky, they twinkle bright,
Melodies play through the endless night.
Each star a note, in cosmic tune,
Singing softly of the silver moon.

A rhythmic pulse, the universe wide,
Whispers of secrets, none can hide.
With every glance, a story starts,
Composed quietly by the shivering hearts.

Time drifts on like a fleeting sigh,
Stars twinkle gently, oh so high.
They tell of dreams, of journeys far,
In stillness wrapped, like a shining scar.

Underneath their serene embrace,
Hope ignites in the darkest place.
A symphony of silent art,
Echoing deep within the heart.

The Breath of a Frozen Dawn

Whispers of frost dance in the air,
Glistening sunlight meets the chill's stare.
Each crystal sparkles on the branch,
Nature awakens, a silent romance.

Morning's breath, a soft, gentle sigh,
Under the veil of a cobalt sky.
Stillness holds as the world comes alive,
In the heart of winter, hope will thrive.

Footsteps crunch on the powdered ground,
In the stillness, a magic is found.
Winter's canvas, painted with grace,
A fleeting moment, a frozen embrace.

Birds take flight, their song fills the void,
Nature’s harmony, delicately enjoyed.
The dawn unfolds in ethereal light,
Wrapped in warmth, surrender to night.

Radiance of a Snow-blanketed World

A blanket of white covers the earth,
Silent beauty, a moment of worth.
Trees stand tall, their branches adorned,
Under the weight of a winter reborn.

Sunrise breaks, casting shadows long,
In the stillness, hear the world’s song.
Every flake dances, each one unique,
Nature's attire, so pure, so meek.

Footprints trail in the shimmering light,
A journey carved through the soft bite.
Frozen rivers reflect the sky’s hue,
Radiance glimmers, a stunning view.

Children laughing, joy fills the air,
Snowmen rising without a care.
The magic of winter, alive and bright,
Whispers of warmth in the cold, clear night.

Lost in the Harmony of Cold

In the quiet, where shadows play,
Nature's melody guides the way.
Frosted whispers in twilight's glow,
A symphony written in flakes of snow.

Echoes of winter weave through the trees,
Songs of the cold, carried by the breeze.
The stillness sings a lullaby sweet,
A hushed serenade, where two worlds meet.

Stars twinkle in an indigo sea,
Frozen dreams wrapped in reverie.
Each breath, a promise, a tale untold,
In the silence profound, warmth takes hold.

Evening’s embrace, a soft, silken shawl,
Cradling the earth, answering its call.
Lost in the harmony, hearts entwined,
In the chill of the night, solace we find.

Melodies of the Enchanted Night

Under the blanket of a starry veil,
The world transforms, a beautiful tale.
Moonlight dances on the frost-kissed ground,
In the silence, magic can be found.

Whispers of winter, soft and light,
Carry the secrets of the night.
Each flake a note in the evening's song,
Inviting dreams where we all belong.

The air hangs thick with mystery,
As shadows waltz, setting spirits free.
In the stillness, hearts begin to soar,
Unraveling joy, forevermore.

Nature breathes in a rhythmic flow,
Guiding the stars in a radiant glow.
As darkness settles, the night ignites,
In the enchantment, find love’s delights.

Shadows of the Frosted Trees

Beneath the moon's gentle glow,
Silent whispers of night flow.
Branches heavy with icy grace,
Shadows dance in a still space.

Frozen dreams in the cold air,
Nature's beauty, beyond compare.
In the hush of the winter's song,
Echoes linger, sweet and strong.

Softly, the world seems to rest,
Wrapped in white, nature's best.
Frosted limbs reaching wide,
Hiding secrets deep inside.

Yet in this silent embrace,
Life waits, ready to trace.
With dawn's light soon to arise,
Frost will kiss the darkened skies.

A Symphony of Shimmering White

Snowflakes twirl in the crisp air,
Soft melodies everywhere.
Each one unique, a fleeting sight,
Dancing down, pure and bright.

A blanket of calm on the ground,
Where laughter and joy abound.
Children's dreams in the cold play,
As winter's charm holds sway.

Whispers of winds weave through trees,
Nature's song, a gentle tease.
In the echo of winter's breath,
Life deepens, revealing depth.

Crisp air fills with the sound,
Of every heart that's unbound.
In a world dressed in white,
Hope glimmers with pure delight.

The Breath of a Frosty Dawn

Morning breaks with a silent sigh,
Underneath a pale blue sky.
Frost clings tight to every blade,
Nature's canvas artfully laid.

The stillness speaks of new day's start,
Whispers fill the waking heart.
Sunrise paints the icy scene,
Warmth awaits where dreams have been.

Golden rays begin to pierce,
Through the chill that feels so fierce.
Nature stirs with soft intent,
Embers of warmth, a day well spent.

Every breath we take so clear,
Frosty trails where we wander near.
In moments caught between the beat,
Life unfolds in its retreat.

Dreams Wrapped in Snow

Under blankets, dreams take flight,
Frosted lace, a pure delight.
Crystals twinkle like the stars,
Holding wishes, near and far.

Each flake tells a story bound,
In silence, magic can be found.
Children dream of lands afar,
Painting worlds where wonders are.

Amidst the hush, hearts beat slow,
In the warmth of the winter's glow.
Memories wrapped in layers tight,
Each one shimmering in the night.

With every step, the hush will grow,
As dreams unfurl beneath the snow.
Footprints lead us on this quest,
Where hope and memory find their rest.

Fragments of Ice and Light

Crystal shards dance in the air,
Reflecting whispers of the cold.
Each flake a story, unique and rare,
In silence, their fate unfolds.

The sun flickers, a golden eye,
Catching secrets in its gaze.
Through delicate patterns they drift and fly,
In the twilight’s soft embrace.

Underneath a blanket of white,
The world breathes, a quiet share.
A moment captured, pure delight,
In the stillness, we find our prayer.

Each fragment glimmers, sparks the soul,
A reminder of time's gentle flight.
Together they weave, they make us whole,
In the dance of ice and light.

So let us cherish, hold them dear,
These fleeting forms of nature’s art.
In the heart’s chamber, we keep them near,
Fragments of ice, fragments of heart.

A Canvas of White Dreams

Softly brushed with winter's hand,
The earth lies wrapped in silence deep.
A canvas waits, untouched and grand,
Where thoughts and whispers gently creep.

The horizon glows with muted hues,
As clouds drift lazily above.
In this realm, imagination brews,
A world painted with dreams of love.

Footsteps echo on paths untread,
As snowflakes fall in graceful arcs.
Each print a story that's softly said,
Leaving behind its fleeting marks.

In the stillness, visions fly,
A tapestry of hope and light.
With every breath, the dreams comply,
Creating life from winter's night.

So let the snow weave tales anew,
As stars peek through the velvet sky.
In this canvas, pure and true,
We find the courage to dream, to try.

Bare Branches, Softly Sighing

In the quiet of the twilight hour,
Bare branches stretch, reaching wide.
They whisper secrets to the flower,
In the dusk, where wonders hide.

Softly sighing with the breeze,
Each limb a story, etched in time.
They dance and sway with graceful ease,
In every moment, every chime.

The world around fades into night,
Stars awaken, twinkling bright.
In the shadows, dreams take flight,
Carried softly on the light.

Though stripped of leaves, their beauty glows,
A testament of strength and grace.
In winter's clutch, hope still flows,
Finding warmth in every space.

So let us learn from branches bare,
To stand resilient through the chill.
In silent strength, we share and care,
Softly sighing, we find our will.

Glacial Rhythms of the Heart

In frozen depths, the heart beats slow,
A glacial rhythm, steady and true.
Through quiet layers, emotions flow,
Each pulse a whisper, old yet new.

Beneath the frost, a warmth resides,
Like molten rivers, hidden bright.
In stark stillness, the spirit glides,
Finding solace in the night.

Time unfolds like the melting snow,
Revealing paths unseen before.
In each drop, the heart will grow,
In winter's grasp, we learn to soar.

With every thaw, new life awaits,
A dance of hope in cold embrace.
Through glacial rhythms, true love creates,
A journey worth the time and space.

So let the heart, like ice, be free,
To change, to bend, and to renew.
In every beat, let it decree,
The glacial dance of me and you.

Lullabies of the Lonesome Hearth

In the quiet of the night,
Whispers dance, soft and light.
Embers glow with tender grace,
Shadows flicker in their place.

Dreams entwine on gentle sighs,
Wrapped in warmth beneath the skies.
Echoes of a distant song,
Where the heartbeats still belong.

Hope is kindled in the dark,
A flame that leaves its gentle mark.
Comfort found in tender gleam,
As memories weave through the dream.

Time drips slowly like the dew,
Each moment cherished, strong and true.
In the stillness, stories stir,
Lullabies of love confer.

Underneath the blanket's fold,
Lies the warmth against the cold.
In soft corners, life retains,
Lullabies whisper through the panes.

Glimmering Paths in the Cold

Footprints glisten on the ground,
By the stars, a tale is found.
Moonlight drapes a silver veil,
Guiding hearts through frost and pale.

Nature hums a gentle tune,
Underneath the watchful moon.
Winds weave soft with every stride,
Drawing dreams from the night tide.

Branches creak with whispered night,
Sparkling under pale starlight.
Each breath fogs in frosty air,
Yet the path is bright and fair.

Laughter lingers, pure and bright,
With every step, a dance of light.
Together, onward we will tread,
Through the chill where hearts are led.

In the cold, we share our glow,
Glimmers dance, and life will flow.
Hand in hand, we chase the dawn,
Finding warmth as dreams are drawn.

Frost-Kissed Memories

Whispers of the past arise,
Frost-kissed dreams beneath the skies.
Each moment held within a sigh,
Frozen time that will not die.

Laughter echoes in the air,
Memories wrapped in winter's care.
Images painted with soft light,
In a world that's dressed in white.

Beneath the snow, the flowers wait,
Silent stories, rich with fate.
In the cold, we find our peace,
Frost-kissed memories never cease.

Time unveils its gentle grace,
In every line, a soft embrace.
In the chill, we hold so dear,
Frosted moments, crystal clear.

Through the trees, the shadows play,
Guiding us along the way.
In the heart, their warmth will stay,
Frost-kissed memories here to stay.

The Frozen Canvas of Time

In a world of white and blue,
Time stands still, moments ensue.
Each flake falls a fleeting rhyme,
A masterpiece of frozen time.

Brush strokes of the winter chill,
Painting life upon the hill.
Silent whispers fill the air,
In this canvas, hearts lay bare.

Every glance, a story told,
In the frost, all dreams unfold.
Wonders dance in icy gleam,
As we wander through the dream.

Tales are woven, soft and light,
In the stillness of the night.
Every heartbeat, every sigh,
On this canvas, we comply.

In the frost, our spirits blend,
Moments captured, hearts transcend.
Through the cold, we find a sign,
Life's true essence, frozen time.

Harmonies in the Stillness

In twilight’s soft embrace we find,
Whispers of the night unwind.
The world rests blissfully still,
Awaiting dreams our hearts will fill.

Stars twinkle in the velvet skies,
Nature breathes with tender sighs.
Moments linger like sweet wine,
In this peace, our souls align.

Echoes dance on gentle air,
Silhouettes of love lay bare.
Silent wishes, hopes arise,
In stillness, joy never dies.

Together in this sacred space,
We find our dreams, we find our grace.
Harmony within our reach,
In the stillness, life will teach.

Shadows play on tranquil streams,
Carrying our softest dreams.
In twilight's arms, we’ll stay awhile,
Wrapped in peace, in nature’s smile.

Icy Serenades Underneath the Moon

Beneath the moon’s pale shining light,
Icy whispers fill the night.
Frozen melodies softly flow,
Harmonies in winter’s glow.

Snowflakes twirl like dancers free,
Nature’s song in symphony.
Chilling breaths in silver air,
A serenade of love laid bare.

Crystals glisten on the trees,
Carrying the softest freeze.
Each note drifts through the cold,
Stories of the brave and bold.

Night but cloaks the tales of old,
In its grasp, our hearts unfold.
Icy serenades call us near,
Underneath the moon, we hear.

In the frost, we find our song,
Where the cold and dreams belong.
Together, let us dance and sway,
In moonlit nights, forever stay.

Frost's Gentle Caress

Morning breaks with a tender touch,
Frost's gentle caress speaks much.
Glistening fields, a sparkling sight,
Nature wrapped in soft, white light.

Each blade whispers a muted tune,
Beneath the watchful, glowing moon.
Cold embraces hearts that yearn,
In frosty air, the world will turn.

Frosted petals on silvery ground,
Echoing the beauty found.
A soothing hush, a calming breath,
In this stillness, we find depth.

Embracing winter's quiet grace,
We cherish time and space.
With every chill, warmth will return,
As seasons shift, our spirits churn.

In frost's arms, we find our peace,
Where worries fade and fears decrease.
Nature's art in every guise,
Frost's gentle caress never lies.

Shadows of Ice-bound Memories

In shadows deep where whispers creep,
Ice-bound memories softly seep.
Echoes of laughter, moments shared,
Frozen in time, hearts laid bare.

Each flake a tale of yesterdays,
In winter's grasp, the spirit sways.
Shadows dance on frosty ground,
In silence, our pasts are found.

Ghostly figures in the frost,
Remind us of what was lost.
Yet in the chill, warmth still breathes,
In icy realms where memory weaves.

Through bitter cold, hope does spark,
Guiding souls out of the dark.
Shadows dwindle, truth emerges,
In ice-bound lore, our heart surges.

As seasons change and light unfolds,
We discover the warmth that golds.
In every shadow, love will stay,
In ice-bound memories, we find our way.

A Ballad of Infinite White

In the silence where snowflakes dance,
All is wrapped in a gentle trance.
Whispers low in the winter night,
Drifting dreams in ethereal light.

Mountains guard the secrets told,
Frosty tales of the brave and bold.
Each flake a story, a moment held,
In the heart of winter, where magic swelled.

Frosted trees wear garments fine,
Beneath the stars, their branches shine.
A canvas pure, the world so bright,
Infinite beauty cloaked in white.

Echoes of laughter, a child's delight,
Slide down hills in the moonlit night.
In this realm where cold winds blow,
A ballad of white forever flows.

As dawn ascends with a blush of rose,
The world awakens from silent doze.
Yet in the heart, the chill remains,
A ballad of winter, forever reigns.

Threads of Ice in the Sky

Under the heavens, a tapestry vast,
Threads of ice in the clouds are cast.
Silver lace drapes the twilight hue,
Whispers of winter, old yet new.

Tiny crystals twinkle like stars,
Painting the night with frosty bars.
Every shimmer a story spun,
Illuminated dreams 'till the morning sun.

The moon casts shadows on frozen streams,
Where the world lies asleep in frozen dreams.
Branches bow down with a weight so light,
Captured in splendor, a stunning sight.

Frozen echoes in the evening's peace,
Nature's artwork that will never cease.
In this moment, a quiet sigh,
Threads of ice weave through the sky.

Beneath the chill, behold the grace,
Nature adorned in a frozen lace.
A dance of light, bright and spry,
Threads of ice in the darkened sky.

Glistening Shadows of the Dusk

As twilight falls with a gentle sigh,
Glistening shadows in colors fly.
Softly they weave through the ancient trees,
Carried away on the whispering breeze.

In the hush of eve, the world turns still,
Fading embers of daylight's thrill.
Moonlight shimmers on the icy ground,
Enchanting beauty where dreams are found.

The night awakens, a canvas divine,
Silver threads where the stars align.
Every shadow tells a tale untold,
Of wishes granted and hearts made bold.

Beneath the glimmer of the night's embrace,
Life slows down to make its space.
In dusk's sweet glow, the magic grows,
Glistening shadows, where wonder flows.

With each heartbeat, the night expands,
Cradled softly in celestial hands.
In this moment, the world feels right,
Glistening shadows in the fading light.

The Beauty of Cold Embrace

In winter’s grasp, a quiet grace,
The beauty lies in cold embrace.
A crystalline world awaits our gaze,
Wrapped in silence, a tender haze.

Frost-kissed branches dance in line,
Painting portraits, divine design.
Each breath a mist on the frozen air,
In winter’s clutch, we feel the care.

Softly falling, the snowflakes glide,
Each one unique, a magic ride.
In the chill, our spirits soar,
Finding warmth in the cold once more.

The stillness sings as shadows grow,
Time slows down in a gentle flow.
In chilly nights under stars that blaze,
We discover joy in cold embrace.

So let us wander through this white,
Where beauty dances in the night.
For in the hush of winter's space,
We find our hearts in cold embrace.

Frosty Trails of Time

Footprints frozen in the snow,
Whispers of the winds that blow,
Each step a story left behind,
In the chill, new paths we find.

Icicles hang from branches high,
Glistening under a pale sky,
Time stands still, the world in white,
Memories dance in the soft light.

The air is crisp, the world is clear,
In winter's grasp, we feel no fear,
With every breath, the magic grows,
As silent beauty gently flows.

Shadows stretch as daylight fades,
The twilight calls, a soft cascade,
Stars emerge in the evening chill,
Nature rests, its heart so still.

In frost's embrace, dreams find their place,
Time weaves slowly in this space,
With every heartbeat, winter shines,
In frosty trails of ancient signs.

Reflections of an Icy Heart

In the mirror of the frozen lake,
Ripples shimmer, gently shake,
A heart encased in crystal clear,
Whispers of longing draw so near.

Winter's breath, a frosty sigh,
Nature's pulse begins to cry,
Within the chill, emotions freeze,
A tender ache upon the breeze.

Beneath the surface, warmth hides deep,
Secrets buried where shadows creep,
Time will thaw the layers bright,
Unveiling love, igniting light.

As snowflakes fall, a soft embrace,
The icy heart begins to trace,
The warmth of hope, a gentle spark,
In winter's night, we find our mark.

Reflections shimmer, truth unfolds,
In frozen moments, stories told,
An icy heart learns to feel,
In a world so wondrous and surreal.

The Spirit of the Silent Season

Beneath the snow, the earth lies still,
Nature pauses, a quiet thrill,
In hibernation, dreams take flight,
The spirit stirs in the soft night.

Whispers linger on the air,
Stories told without a care,
Silent echoes wrap the land,
The spirit moves, a gentle hand.

Frosted branches, a lacework fine,
Under moonlight, they intertwine,
With every breath, the world slows down,
In winter's cloak, peace can be found.

The stars above twinkle like fire,
In this stillness, hearts conspire,
To dream of warmer days ahead,
While embracing the chill instead.

The spirit dances in the night,
Guiding us with soft, warm light,
In winter's arms, we find our grace,
The silent season's sweet embrace.

Songs of the Winter Night

In the quiet of the evening glow,
A melody drifts on winds that blow,
The songs of winter softly call,
Echoes of magic that enthrall.

Beneath the stars, the world is bright,
As shadows play in the pale moonlight,
Each note a whisper, gentle and clear,
Songs of the season, hearts draw near.

The fire crackles, warmth surrounds,
In the silence, joy abounds,
Through frosted panes, we hear the tune,
Of a winter night, beneath the moon.

Snowflakes dance in the brisk night air,
A symphony woven with utmost care,
In every flake, a story's spun,
As winter's ballad has begun.

So let us gather by the flame,
And sing the songs that bear our name,
In the heart of winter's gentle light,
We'll find our solace in the night.

Beneath the Blanket of Soft White

Snowflakes fall, a silent song,
Hiding streets where we belong.
Each breath brings a warming light,
Beneath the blanket of soft white.

Trees wear coats of crystal sheen,
Moonlight bathes the world in dream.
Footprints trace a gentle path,
In this land of winter's wrath.

Whispers dance on frosty air,
Laughter echoes, free from care.
Children sledding down the hill,
Winter's laughter, crisp and chill.

Inside, a fire's golden glow,
Stories shared, time moving slow.
Hot cocoa warms our weary hands,
Joyful hearts, as love expands.

Under stars that brightly gleam,
We find warmth in every dream.
Together in this winter's heart,
Finding bliss, we will not part.

Winter's Haiku

Frosted windowpanes,
Whispering winds tell stories,
Winter's breath lingers.

Silent snowflakes fall,
Cloaking the earth in stillness,
Nature's lullaby.

Moonlight on the hill,
Shadows dance beneath the trees,
A chill in the air.

Embers softly glow,
Crackling warmth beside the fire,
Comfort wrapped in light.

A seasonal pause,
Time to reflect, to savor,
Winter fills our hearts.

A Serenade of Frost and Fire

Beneath the stars, a frosty night,
Crackling flames, a warm delight.
Whispers blend with nature's sigh,
Together, fire and frost comply.

Snowflakes shimmer, twinkling bright,
Bright as embers in the night.
Cupped in hands, hot chocolate flows,
Savoring warmth as the cold wind blows.

Beneath the pines, the shadows play,
In the glow of twilight gray.
The world transformed, in crisp embrace,
Frost and fire, a soft interlace.

In harmony, they reignite,
Passionate hearts in winter's bite.
Songs of joy in every crack,
Together strong, we'll not look back.

With each frost, the fire's lore,
A serenade that we adore.
In every heartbeat, warmth and peace,
Together, may our love increase.

Celestial Dance of the Long Night

Stars alight in velvet sky,
Moonbeams whisper, softly sigh.
Winter's chill wraps all around,
In silence, dreams are gently found.

The night unfolds a tale so grand,
Cosmic wonders, hand in hand.
As time slows, we drift and sway,
In the magic of this ballet.

Frost-kissed landscapes gleam and glow,
Light of heaven's endless flow.
Each twinkle holds a thousand dreams,
In winter's grip, all more than seems.

Together beneath the stars,
We share whispers, close to ours.
In awe of beauty, we entwine,
This celestial dance is yours and mine.

As dawn approaches, shadows creep,
Night's embrace, forever deep.
Yet in our hearts, the stars remain,
A promise made in winter's reign.

The Quiet of Falling Snow

Whispers drift from sky to ground,
Blanketing the world around.
Each flake dances in soft grace,
Time slows down in this embrace.

Pine trees wear a frosted crown,
Nature hushes, settles down.
Footsteps muffled, secrets keep,
In the stillness, silence deep.

Moonlight glimmers on the white,
Stars twinkle in the frosty night.
A peaceful aura fills the air,
A calm moment, free from care.

Children's laughter breaks the peace,
Winter's joy will never cease.
Snowmen stand with grinning glee,
While snowflakes swirl and dance so free.

The world transformed, a sight to see,
In the quiet, hearts agree.
Nature's canvas, pure and bright,
Wrapped in winter's soft, sweet light.

A Tale of Crystal Breeze

Winds whisper secrets, soft and clear,
Carrying tales for all to hear.
Beneath the branches, shadows play,
Where the icy crystals sway.

A dance of sparks in morning sun,
Frozen drapes where rivers run.
Each breath of air feels sharp and bright,
Bringing life to wintry light.

Snowflakes twirl like tiny stars,
Marking paths of silver scars.
Through frosty woods, the stories glide,
On the crystal breeze they ride.

Listen close to nature’s song,
In the cold, where we belong.
Every gust a fleeting trace,
Whispers echo, leave no space.

In the stillness, dreams take flight,
Carried forth by crystal light.
A tale spun in the frost’s embrace,
A world transformed, a sacred space.

Hushed Voices in the Cold

In the hush of twilight's glow,
Voices soft, like falling snow.
Whispers fill the frozen air,
Secret stories linger there.

Fires crackle, embers shine,
Hearts entwined in the divine.
Each word spoken, warm and bold,
Wrapped in layers from the cold.

Footsteps crunch on winter's floor,
Echoes of what came before.
Moments treasured, shared with cheer,
In the cold, we hold them near.

Snowflakes flutter, silent prayer,
Binding souls in frosty air.
Hope takes flight in glowing light,
As day turns into velvet night.

In that stillness, truths unfold,
Hushed voices speak when nights are cold.
A tapestry of warmth they weave,
In the quiet, we believe.

Midnight Murmurs of Ice

Underneath the watchful moon,
Midnight murmurs start to croon.
Icy whispers through the trees,
Carried on the frozen breeze.

Stars like diamonds, bright and cold,
Casting stories, yet untold.
In this stillness, dreams arise,
Wrapped in winter's sweet disguise.

Frosted windows, curtains drawn,
Nighttime hums a gentle song.
Peaceful moments, hearts align,
In the chill, our spirits shine.

Laughter dances, spirits soar,
Echoes heard forevermore.
As shadows play, the world stands still,
In midnight's arms, we find our will.

Cold and quiet, yet so alive,
In the icy silence, we thrive.
Murmurs blend with dreams of light,
In winter's embrace, we take flight.

www.ingramcontent.com/pod-product-compliance
Ingram Content Group UK Ltd.
Pitfield, Milton Keynes, MK11 3LW, UK
UKHW031939151224
452382UK00006B/283

9 789916 793817